The Start-Up
ENTREPRENEUR

The Start-Up
ENTREPRENEUR

An Emerging Market Experience

SOLA SOLARIN

authorHOUSE®

AuthorHouse™ UK
1663 Liberty Drive
Bloomington, IN 47403 USA
www.authorhouse.co.uk
Phone: 0800.197.4150

Published by AuthorHouse 10/27/2015

ISBN: 978-1-5049-9280-0 (sc)
ISBN: 978-1-5049-9279-4 (hc)
ISBN: 978-1-5049-9281-7 (e)

Print information available on the last page.

This book is printed on acid-free paper.

This book is dedicated to the best life decision I ever made: my greatest investment still yielding returns that are at once invaluable and inexhaustible; my greatest champion and cheer leader, my superstar, my friend—my wife, Enitan.

Contents

Chapter 1

Introduction

Nigeria conjures up different images and different emotions in different people. To other Africans, it is a country of very loud or assertive people, depending on their frame of reference. To the world at large, it is a nation of confident, football-loving, aggressive, and friendly people. Nigeria has of late also been defined by article 419 of the Nigerian Criminal Code (the section of the code that deals with advance-fee fraud, and therefore a cognomen for the typical Nigerian email promising you huge wealth for just providing your bank details) and Nollywood (the Nigerian film industry). To the Nigerian himself or herself, it is a place to flee from, a country that is perpetually underperforming and lawless. It is a graveyard of many businesses.

But the reality is slightly different. My consulting business frequently reports on the Nigerian business environment, and despite the angry rhetoric you hear from Nigerians on a daily basis, there are certain facts you can't ignore. Up to 2014, Nigeria was consistently in the top ten fastest growing economies for eight years. It has a resilient economy and was barely fazed by the global meltdown of 2008. The management of the headwind caused by the global economic meltdown of that year was helped by a comfortable foreign reserve, huge savings in what is called its excess crude account (ECA), and a competent economic management team. The country has also been fairly rewarded with a consistent above-average grade by the rating agencies and with good pricing of the country's foreign bond.

Nigeria returns some of the highest profit margins to businesses in construction, oil and gas, telecommunications, and financial services.

The infrastructure of Nigeria, however, makes businesses with no protection against foreign competition very weak, and such businesses record very high mortality.

While studying for my master of business administration (MBA) degree, I had to analyze and discuss with my classmates more than 500 business cases. What I learnt from that experience was that there is no problem that any business in Nigeria is confronting that had never been faced and resolved by people in other countries. The convenient phrase in Nigeria that 'nothing works' is simply an excuse for failure to dispassionately interrogate the challenges of the business and apply the right remedies. I always tell people that abandoning a business where you cannot compete could be the correct remedy instead of blaming and cursing everybody else.

During the early 1990s when Nigerians thought that a 75 per cent inflation rate was hellish, we discussed cases of businesses in Brazil and Mexico that survived a 1200 per cent inflation rate during the same period.

This book is a narrative about my adventures running small businesses in Nigeria and thoughts on how to make a success of it.

Chapter 2

The decision

The decision to be an entrepreneur often is not a deliberate one. It is sometimes forced by circumstances: a fruitless search for a new job, or the loss of one. It may also represent the desire to escape from a dead-end job.

Mine was a constellation of triggers. I had always wanted to be the head of a big manufacturing company – picturing the constant whine of production equipment, the steady stream of steam from the exhaust of boilers, the quiet but busy efficiency of people darting in and out of offices or hunched over thick files or seated around a conference table discussing life and death issues of business. I thought it would be the perfect life for me to be at the head of such a business. However, staying in a company for thirty years climbing the corporate ladder would be too long a road and one strewed with too many mines and stumbling blocks. The top job is never assured. In the ten years I spent in a multinational pharmaceutical company, the business split once, did one acquisition, and a merger. All of these are corporate events of seismic proportions and can upturn any well-laid plan. Job security is therefore a myth, and no formula guarantees success on the corporate climb.

Coming to a decision about entrepreneurship is not an easy thing. It is at once personal and grave. The most difficult aspect is the mental conditioning to, and unwavering conviction in, the belief that it is what you want to do. You are about to forego the regularity and security (that word again?) of a monthly pay cheque when you likely have to contend with the stubborn regularity of expenses that have to be met: mortgage/rent payments, housekeeping expenses, school fees, and a sundry of other obligations that the monthly salary assures. A breach of that order is difficult to contemplate for a mind attuned to a monthly salary sequence. The decision may also only be made more difficult by well-wishers, colleagues, friends, and family members who see the peril in the disappearance of a predictable and stable income stream.

You certainly need the buy-in of your spouse, children, and other close family to make the decision to entrepreneurship. The first difficult sale you will need to do is convincing this set of people that the entrepreneurship route is one that you've carefully considered and that the choice is one you have deliberately made and the challenge is one that you are ready to embrace.

However convinced you are about your entrepreneurial journey, the true test of its viability is your ability to sell it to third parties. There will be many doubters and naysayers. I will advise that you listen to their stories. If they raise serious but cogent reasons for why they have doubts, take in their viewpoints and use them to refine your plans and your strategy. Your plan needs all the knocks it can attract. You will get better educated, and your conviction about the project will be better strengthened.

Chapter 3

Timing

There is a school of thought that believes that you should commence your private business while in paid employment. The argument is that the paid employment helps in maintaining an income stream before the business picks up steam and becomes self-sustaining. I have never subscribed to this school of thought. Apart from the obvious ethical conflict in sharing your time between two businesses when your employer is paying for and therefore has a right to your undivided attention, a start-up business is a twenty-four hour job and requires all of your resources to get it going. Besides, to adopt an attitude where one does not dip both toes in is a pointer to the fact that two traits that are critical to the survival of your business are still lacking: conviction and courage.

The few things you do about your new business while in paid employment should be limited to incorporating the business, setting up the office, and designing your stationeries.

The requirement for courage in entrepreneurship suggests that there is a large dose of risk involved in taking on the challenge of entrepreneurship. All of the questions you have about the venture will not have been answered, all of the resources you need will not be available, and, in fact, you will have a bit of self-doubt about your capacity as an individual to make a success of it. It doesn't matter what your background is. Whether you are a fresh graduate with no experience at all or a very experienced retired CEO this situation will arise and persist, and the depth of it is only a matter of degree. Therefore, if you think that private enterprise is the future you want to create for yourself, the time to start is now. Give yourself a deadline, draft your resignation letter, and submit it. Then you have crossed the river, and burnt the bridge. There is no retreat, no surrender. Your new life begins.

I started my journey in entrepreneurship by abruptly resigning from the CEO position of a health maintenance organization (HMO). Prior to that job, I had been with a multinational pharmaceutical company and had been preparing for private enterprise. I had moved to a new house that can double as an office. I had saved some money and resourced my house with the basic requirements of a business, including a telephone (a big deal in the year 1996 when mobile phones were not freely available in Nigeria), a computer, a printer, and basic office furniture.

My sojourn with the HMO was to get a feel of the leadership of a business. The experience helped a bit. It revealed that the CEO position was just a title; it was just another employee position without the freedom to experiment with your ideas and the regular adrenalin rush that the position of an owner/manager exposes you to.

Resigning from that position compelled me to spend every moment thinking of how to progress my private company. It took another six months before we booked our first cash receipt.

Chapter 4

Plan for It

While an entrepreneurial venture may appear like an impulsive and reckless act, for it to be successful it must be carefully thought through. It may not be subjected to the rigour of KPMG (providing professional audit, tax, and advisory services) or an Accenture (and you probably don't have those kind of resources anyway), but it will be nice if you can sit over drinks with a strategy consultant who will help you tick the boxes, and answer questions like: What business are you doing? How big is the market? Who are your competitors? How is the market segmented? Is the market growing? What is the profit margin like? What is the interplay of suppliers, customers, barriers to entry, and barriers to exit, and how do they affect competition in the market? What confers competitive advantage in the market? What will be your unique selling proposition? What competitive strength will you leverage, and how will you build it? What is your family's cash need, and will the business generate enough cash to finance your lifestyle now and in the future? It is very important that you project your cash flow for the first year of the business, and discuss it with a few trusted people.

Listen carefully to people's comments, and it will be easy for you to know which ones to accept and which ones to discard. All of them will make you wiser.

Chapter 5

Which business?

The economy of Nigeria has its own peculiarities, chief among which is lack of seed money and long-term capital for start-ups. There is also a social and legal environment that does not make enforcement of contracts very easy if not making them out right impossible. For an entrepreneur, therefore, deciding on a business to start will have to factor in these realities.

You should start with businesses that you can commence with resources that are within easy reach like your savings, and the little you can borrow from friends and family. Service businesses and consultancies fall into this category. They require little capital investment, and you can start the business from the boot of your car. Or if you need anything more elaborate, from the office of a friend.

A different category of business that is suited for the Nigerian financial architecture is those with a quick cash cycle of less than three months. Three-month financing is very much available with finance houses, microfinance banks, individuals, and even banks. Businesses that fit in these categories will be mainly trading, and services that stretch for a month or two, such as interior decoration, leasehold improvements, and a sundry of others. It's no surprise, therefore, that Nigeria's gross domestic product (GDP) is dominated by businesses like distributive trade, construction, and financial services that can accommodate low capital investment, a quick cash cycle, and short-term financing.

An entrepreneur will probably start in an industry he or she has thorough knowledge of and in which he or she has developed a rich network of contacts.

Another category of businesses that are often ignored are those that are already distressed and that are being liquidated. A list of these can easily be obtained from the legal departments of banks, and financial services companies and law firms specializing in receivership and insolvencies. There is an association of insolvency practitioners, and they can easily serve as a link to all of their members and businesses that may be available for sale.

A good indicator of under-served sectors are products or services that people are willing to pay in advance for like real estate, or at some point in the recent past, fuel for power generators.

Some entrepreneurs have even advised going around with a pencil and a pocket notebook and jotting down every poor service or irritation experienced in the course of the day. If you think you are capable of doing better or providing the service, then you have a potential business in your hand.

Chapter 6

Raising money

In Nigeria, starting out fresh in business is a factor against your ability to raise money from where it ought to be freely available: the banks. Although banks engage in the riskiest of businesses, that is, giving credit, they are in fact wired to be risk averse. Here you are, with no pedigree in running a business and submitting an untested business for financing by a bank. No bank on the feasibility of your business and your pedigree (or lack of it in business) will give you money, except of course if you have collateral in a cash deposit with the bank or top-grade property in Abuja or Lagos.

More so, for a new business what you are looking for is patient capital that is quasi-equity (that is, the category of <u>debt</u> taken on by a <u>company</u> that has some features of <u>equity</u>, such as being <u>unsecured</u>) – the kind of capital that will probably stay in the business for life. For this kind of capital, you will probably draw on your savings, reach out to close friends and family members who will be patient until the business can pay back the loan or not be disinclined to converting the debt to equity.

It is also important that you are very conservative in your deployment of cash. Cash is scarce and expensive. The less of it that you deploy the better it will be for your business starting out. One thing I found most helpful is thinking more in terms of what resources I want to acquire with the cash, rather than being fixated on the cash itself. You should rigorously interrogate every item on your cash flow projection and ask whether you can borrow the relevant amount of cash from somebody. If you decide that you cannot, ask whether you can lease it for the particular period that you need it. If you decide that you must invest in the ownership, consider whether you can share it with somebody else. These sorts of questions can be revealing. All of a sudden you may find that what you need an office for is just the occasional visit by clients, and you can anticipate that being not more than twice a month. You may consider talking to a friend or family member to use his or her business premises and his or her meeting room for these occasional visits.

If you do determine that an office is critical to your business, you could still consider all of your available options, such as leasing a big house that can double as both your residence and office or sharing an office with a business that is not in competition with yours or is even complementary to yours.

Your cleaning business can operate out of your garage, and you can hire cleaning equipment and cleaners for specific contracts. You can then devote your time and resources to the most critical metrics in the business, that is, getting contracts, ensuring that a quality job is done, and chasing payments.

My pharmaceutical product development and marketing business also exploited the excess capacity in the industry to start out very lean. We focused on reading the market for opportunities and designing products that infrastructure in the Nigerian pharmaceutical industry can handle. While avoiding the heavy outlay in investment a manufacturing infrastructure and the long time all the certifications will take, We were able to enter the market faster and focus on brand building and stock availability. These are the most important factors for success in the pharmaceutical industry.

Chapter 7

Going it alone or partnership

Every entrepreneurial venture owes its existence to the vision and drive of one person. But the project is often so formidable and so huge that a second person can help with launching it and keeping it on an even keel.

People will point at Jim Ovia of Zenith Bank Group, Femi Otedola of Fortis Oil, and even Dangote as examples of lone rangers who have made a success of their entrepreneurial projects. They are right. But I would also like to point to the examples of Fola Adeola and Tayo Aderinokun of Guaranty Trust Bank (GTBank) Plc; Aigboje Aig-Imokhuede and Herbert Wigwe of Access Bank plc; and Wale Tinubu, Mofe Boyo, and Jite Okoloko of Oando Plc.

I have experienced both scenarios of going it alone and being in a partnership, and I would recommend a partnership any day. An entrepreneurial venture can be a lonely – and sometimes harrowing – experience. When spirit is low, cash is down, and it appears everything is collapsing around you, having a partner by your side who either validates your thoughts or challenges your premise can be very comforting. A partner who has a different skill set and dissimilar life experiences can offer a perspective that can totally uplift your spirit and renew your enthusiasm. A partner whose fate also depends on the success or failure of the business and sees the business from within cannot embellish facts or 'Photoshop' the picture for any reason.

From the foregoing, the profile of the ideal partner is already emerging. He or she must be a friend and a kindred spirit. He or she must share in the excitement of private enterprise and be ready for the sacrifice that comes with it. It is best if he or she comes with a complementary skill set and a different personality profile. He or she should be somebody whose counsel you value and whose opinion you respect. Most importantly, he or she must be willing to work in the business. A partner who brings solely an equity contribution with eyes purely on future dividend is the worst kind of person to partner with in a start-up. It is better that you bring him or her in as a provider of debt capital and that you work towards paying him or her back when the business stabilizes. If, however, you must bring in equity partners then make sure to limit their shareholding collectively to a minority, reserving majority ownership for the partners working in the business. The challenge to your control of the business can start very early, and you don't want to spend every waking hour fretting about the next board meeting or annual general meeting (AGM) when there are other things that are critical to the viability of the business.

An entrepreneurial venture pans out in one of two directions: either it fares better than you planned, or it fares worse than you projected. However it plays out, equity partners will think that they are being short-changed and you are not giving them commensurate returns on their investment, or you ruined the business because of your incompetence. They can be snippy, rude, and distracting. It is best to avoid then at the start-up phase of your business.

I have a rich experience to share on this. My first venture was the purchase of the assets of a pharmaceutical manufacturing business from a bank. The initiative was mine and a lawyer friend with similar entrepreneurial aspirations and a shared past. He had another venture he was working on, however, and therefore he had no desire to join me in the business. He was working in the bank that was selling the assets of the company. His background was in corporate finance, and he had good experience in credit. I thought he would be a good fit for my manufacturing and marketing background in the nascent business, even from the outside. I was confident that I could handle operations, and that I would rely on him for finance, basically raising money – the area where I was weakest.

It was difficult raising the money to buy the business between the two of us, and that led us to two other people who we thought could come in as equity partners. Their only interest was the anticipated future prosperity that the business would give them based on projections. One of these people had a background in the capital market, which we thought would help with future fund raising. He was a medical doctor with a family background steeped in a culture of entitlement where every resource irrespective of ownership could be appropriated for private gain; with him, money belonging to the government and shareholders or procured through debt can be expropriated with no obligation to pay it back. He was even unwilling to wait for the business to turn a profit before cashing in. He suggested at a time that we procured debt with the assets of the business and share the money. We can always face the challenge from creditors later. The other personwas a former journalist and talented entrepreneur who had made a success of one business. He is a truly provincial and uncouth character with neither refinement nor cultivation. His exposure in the business world and achievement has done little to assuage the feeling of inferiority he has. He sought every opportunity – often times loudly – to affirm that he is a big and important person. He brought this character flaw to the board, and immediately went to town after the board was composed with statements that he owned the business. He in fact had the least shareholding. Every board meeting was a shouting match, often with other members of the board trying to curtail his boast and bombast about being the greatest business manager and the rest of us not knowing what we are doing. Managing his ego was difficult, and the chair of the board was too weak to assert his position.

This was the kind of board that was meeting quarterly to discuss the life and death situation of a business on the ropes. You had to be on the watch for stratagems and plots to further annihilate a company already on its knees. The board was not adding any value at all, and in fact it became the biggest threat to the survival of the business and led to its eventual death.

I invited the wrong people to the board, but that mistake wouldn't have been terminal if I had retained majority holding. There were family members willing to help, and I could have leveraged other sources of funding to turn around the business. It would have required the restructuring of the shareholding and the board. But I could not lead that charge from such a weak position. It became clear that I had to cut my losses, exit the business I had founded and begin again. The business lasted a further six years, was interdicted by the National Agency for Food and Drug Administration and Control (NAFDAC) (a Nigerian government agency under the Federal Ministry of Health). The board and management became guest of the Nigeria Police Special Fraud Unit, and the loud-mouthed director lost tens of millions of naira in pursuit of ego. The experience chastened him a bit, but it worsened his feeling of inferiority.

What is the moral of this story? Retain majority holding in the hands of the promoters of the business, working full-time within the business. If any director gets adventurous, he or she can be curtailed at the board and put in their place.

I have emphasized a lot the need for those with controlling interest to be working full-time in the business. Experience has taught me that whether a business is doing well or doing badly, there will be suspicions. The fact that a business is doing well in terms of profitability or market share does not automatically mean that there is money to share as dividends. As experience of the telecoms industry in Nigeria taught us, the market could be growing so fast that in order to keep up with growth the business will for a considerable period of time be looking for additional cash from existing shareholders when it has been leveraged to the limit. A non-executive director will not feel the pain of growth, but will think the lifestyle of the company's managers is been sustained by his investment in the company. This breeds resentment and sometimes bad blood and a push to upset the board apple cart.

My next collaboration was with a friend and colleague also with a shared past. He has deep and varied experience in financial services regulation and corporate restructuring. His previous work as a regulator and in consulting in financial services exposed him to businesses in distressed situations and the different tools in the Nigerian space available to turn them around. He had handled a lot of stressful and sometimes dangerous assignments in his career as a corporate undertaker and turnaround specialist. He has solid breeding and moral credentials. His training and experience complements my background in production, marketing, and product development. We had tried out a lot of acquisitions in manufacturing and logistics that never crystallized, but the meltdown of the capital market in 2008 threw up an opportunity for a financial services company that we both jointly acquired 87.5 per cent of its shareholding.

We both got involved in management from the beginning, experiencing first-hand the difficult challenge of turning around a distressed business.

All decisions were jointly taken, and we both could see the ebb and flow of cash. We ran the business without taking salaries, and there was never any suspicion about what we were benefiting from individually from the business. There were people who tried to throw a wedge between us by sowing seeds of doubt about the integrity of either of us, but this was, however, easy to dismiss, as both partners partook in the disbursement of funds and in all investment decisions.

The financial services business is a greater challenge by far than the pharmaceutical manufacturing business, but it is, however, easy to embrace this challenge because of the combined resources of the partners and a board and shareholding structure that is conducive to creating lasting value for all stakeholders.

Chapter 8

Staffing the business

I have often engaged in conversation with people about the quality of Nigerian graduates. There is a popular complaint that there is a lack of people of the right quality to fill positions in businesses. However, I also talk to recruitment consultants and businesses that recruit fresh graduates regularly, and they tell me that there is a surfeit of good quality graduates from Nigerian universities for most job positions – the only exceptions being engineering and other technical positions that require post-graduate tutelage or apprenticeship for a mastery of the trade.

In my company, all positions that require post-secondary school education are advertised. There are a lot of online web portals that do it for free, and they have a very extensive reach; you get responses in the hundreds. You shortlist based on established and advertised criteria and then apply basic tests. A test involving writing a 300-word composition and a test for competence in spoken English are standard. I have friends test for technical skills in accounting and information technology (basically proficiency in use of Microsoft Office applications) as appropriate. I have them read a scientific article and test their skills in comprehending and communicating basic scientific ideas. This all takes quite a bit of time and effort, but I have found that it is worth it – as anyone who has experienced recruitment error will testify.

Most small businesses and even medium-sized ones skimp on rigour during the recruitment process and end up with the wrong complement of staff. Everything skates downhill from then on.

What I have found more difficult to test for is attitude: things like taking responsibility, ambition, perseverance, courage, and integrity. My proxy for testing for this is a peek into the background of applicants. I look at whether they have ever been in a position of leadership in school, church, or any social group. I call previous employers and discuss the staff, even after getting a written response to the reference forms we send to them.

Our experience with those who have been through this process has generally been good.

Recruiting good staff is a good beginning. Training them is the more arduous task. For jobs like administration and accounting it is easier, as you can literally look over their shoulder while working and coach them. Selling skills includes classroom training and field training. Marketing staff may not become productive until the third month.

Monthly meetings and annual appraisals are also tools for managing staff for productivity. A small business manager should make sure that they run like clockwork. Notices and agendas should be sent ahead of time. Meetings should start on time and finish on time. It is a way of training staff for soft skills and holding the right attitudes. More importantly, you can use it to strengthen corporate culture by highlighting what is important to the business.

The same attributes of ambition and high standards that qualified good staff to work for you will also prompt them to constantly be looking for greener pastures. You will probably find that your best staff leave first – condemning you to repeat the cycle of recruitment, training, and acculturation. It can sometimes be frustrating, but there are few effective alternatives.

Chapter 9

Using consultants

A start-up will compete in the same market for human and intellectual resources as the biggest companies in the country. Lack of pedigree and the risk of failure make the start-up an unlikely choice for most jobseekers. This is compounded by the fact that those who are brave enough to try it out will easily move on at the first offer from a big corporate. Listing Oando Plc, Guaranty Trust Bank (GTBank) Plc, or Zenith Bank Plc in a profile works for him or her more than saying that they held a top position in Sola and Sons Ltd.

Your employee pool will be stocked with fresh graduates with little experience and itchy feet. You must find a means of assuring that the processes and assets of your business are not vulnerable to shocks from the sudden departure of an otherwise competent and reliable staff.

Consultants are an imperative for a new business. The more important ones across industries are financial services (including tax), information technology, marketing, and operations. You may need to engage a few others, depending on the industry you play in, for example, compliance services in the pharmaceutical industry, legal services in banking and finance, or human resources if you are doing outsourcing.

Consultants bring a rich experience in specific functions and across industries that can be accessed by a small company. The flexibility that comes with using consultants also helps the cash flow of the business. You can engage them for specific tasks, or you can retain them for a long period. You can also easily disengage them if you are not happy with their services. They can send people to fill the void created by the sudden departure of a staff, and they can help with recruiting, training, and induction of new staff members. They help ensure the stability of the business and reduce the vulnerability to shocks.

Picking the right consultant is an arduous task. Because that sector is poorly regulated and has low barrier to entry, people become consultants only at the cost of printing business cards and incorporating the simplest form of business. It is easy to fall into the hands of charlatans who came into that calling out of lack of choice. The bad ones are incompetent; the more dangerous ones lead you down the path of unethical and outright illicit acts – telling you that there is no other way of getting certification or complying with a government regulation except if you pay a bribe. You should always avoid this type.

The rule of thumb for picking a consultant is the bigger, the better. The bigger consultancies have processes and systems that will ensure that you get a quality service whatever the circumstance. They are used to dealing with big, demanding clients and are used to the highest standards of service delivery. The biggest ones may not take your brief because you are small, or you may not be able to afford their fees. However, if fees are the only problem, I would suggest that you negotiate as much as you can rather than compromise on a good consultant.

The second level is small consultancy shops set up by alumni of the big companies. They have imbibed the values of quality service and often the principal will have a rich network of contacts that can help with any problem.

Anything below this level requires very stringent due diligence. You should assess all other consultants like you are assessing a potential employee. Ask for certifications, and, if you have the time, make sure that they are not fake. Ask for references, and check the references. Test for integrity and attitude. Lastly, be coy to give people in this category a retainership. Let them prove themselves first with one-off tasks.

My most enduring good feeling about consultants was our relationship with a communication company called Design Forge. It is the subsidiary of Bates Cosse, one of the six biggest advertising agencies in Nigeria. They designed all our packaging and promotional materials: business cards, pens, notepads and so forth. Apart from helping to clarify my thinking about the marketing strategy for the company and our products, they took me through a checklist of the unique selling proposition, market positioning, the particular market segment to target, pricing, competition, and practically everything that will impact the success of our company and our brand in the market. After my interview with the panel, I was sweaty and feeling good: t type of feeling you have after a good workout at the gym. They converted all of my thoughts to designs and creatives that are still looking beautiful ten years after. They really gave meaning to the phrase 'a thing of beauty is joy forever'.

Another enduring experience – on the negative side – was with a tax consultant. My pharmaceutical product development and marketing company has the auditor also doing our tax returns, and we ensure that we diligently pay all company taxes due every year.

When our auditor now started harassing us for ex gratia payment (a bribe really) to the tax office, I asked why we needed to pay any money to anybody since we were paying all taxes due. He said that it was extortion really, and they would not process our application for a tax clearance certificate if we did not pay the bribe. Worse still, they said that they could send a team to our office for an audit, and there was no way they would not see an infraction of the tax laws. This set me thinking: if you as my consultant cannot keep on the straight and narrow path of conformity with the law and protect us from dubious government officials, why should I keep paying you? I removed the service. The team from the tax office came, and their opening statement was, 'How much are you guys willing to pay us so that we don't waste each other's time?'

The company was blessed with a confident and diligent accountant who kept reassuring me that he didn't see their audit revealing any violation of the law. They stayed for a week, wrote their report and said we had underpaid taxes by a substantial amount relative to our size – bout 10 per cent of our total revenue.

The good thing about the tax law is that the tax auditors have to do a calculation of how they arrive at their figures. However, these tax officials could not come up with anything that we could not defend with documents in our file.

We now called in this tax consultant. His first task was to review all of the documents, do an independent audit, and see if we had not been paying our taxes as due. He came with a verdict that he could defend the level of taxes we had been paying. I now told him to start preparation to represent us at the tax tribunal. He came back much later saying that to get out our tax clearance certificate we needed to pay a bribe of N1m.

I thought, 'What does one have to do to get an honest tax consultant?' We refused to pay the bribe. It generated a lot of written correspondence between us and the tax office. We dropped a hint that we were looking at a resolution by the tax tribunal. Federal Inland Revenue Service (FIRS) officials eventually backed down, released our tax clearance certificate, and never disturbed us again.

This battle cost our little company quite a lot in terms of time, money, and top management effort. But we needed to go through that pass to communicate our values to government officials and learn a lesson about engaging the wrong consultants.

Chapter 10

Corporate culture

What sustains a business forever is its culture. It is the building block of the corporate brand. It is what differentiates your company from competitors. It is the way you do things, and it is the things you don't do. It is what you will hear people say about your company if you were a fly on the wall eavesdropping on their conversation. They are the things you reward staff for doing, and they are the things you punish them for not doing.

I was tuned to corporate cultural issues very early in my career. I started my career with a global company that could not otherwise be effectively controlled except through a very strong cultural orientation. The way in which you dress, the cleanliness of your car, the confidence you display, and the depth of your knowledge are habits that are carefully cultivated to project a particular corporate brand, control behaviour, and ingrain in the heart of the public the minimum they can expect of you. Your culture is managed across the entire business process and interface with the public. Your recruitment process must reflect a bias for people with a cultural fit. Your products and packaging design must project your culture. Your annual appraisal and reward system should reward habits, traits, and other metrics that project corporate culture, and of course sanctions should also be meted out for acts that violate the culture.

The cultural tone of the small business must be set very early at conception by the promoters. It is going to inform the kind of products that you develop, the design of your communication materials, the segment of the market that you are going to play in, your office location, the kind of people you recruit to work for the business, and a plethora of other things.

The small business promoter must cultivate the habit of putting to paper things like the company mission, stating the business you are in and how you want to compete. The vision should state the aspiration of the business and how it wants to be perceived in the market in which it operates.

It is important to also state the company values.

My pharmaceutical product development company has the following as pillars of its culture:

Mission

We are a project-based organization providing innovative solutions to healthcare challenges by connecting different world-class competencies in research, quality, production, and marketing. We solve healthcare problems through brands that communicate our values of trustworthiness, reliability, and efficiency. We are Coriander Resources.

Values

Innovation—We will strive to do things differently by taking on difficult and audacious challenges to provide innovative solutions to real healthcare problems. Our solutions will give value to our customers, the healthcare providers who serve them, the staff, and our shareholders.

Human Resources—People are our most important resource. We take the utmost care to source people that are knowledgeable, talented, and whom subscribe to our virtues of inquisitiveness, trustworthiness, and hard work. We nurture an environment that makes our people professionally fulfilled and reward hard work, innovation, and honesty. We provide training to improve our human capital and promote from within as much as possible.

Profit—Profit for us is our customers' reward for service. We work hard to be deserving of it, knowing that it is a measure of the market's confidence in us and a necessity for business continuity.

All of these efforts will come to naught if the culture is not lived day to day and rigorously managed. The business promoter must be alert to situations or market segments that force them to compromise their values. It will be difficult indeed for a construction company that has chosen to play in the public sector in Nigeria to enforce a culture of ethical and fair dealing.

The company culture also informs the kind of people or businesses to collaborate with. I have made a case for choosing people to partner with in an earlier narrative about the composition of the board of the pharmaceutical manufacturing company. The error still endured after I had left the company. I was lucky that I had made sure to resign from the board of the company since I could no longer vouch for management and oversight the company effectively as a director. In no time, in line with the value orientation of the new board, the company was soon found to be compromising process and quality standards in an industry as sensitive to due process as the pharmaceutical industry. If Nigeria were strict about law enforcement, the directors of the business should be in jail.

The payoff for a strong corporate culture can be really huge. Beyond word-of-mouth affirmation of your credentials by everybody, referrals come on the momentum of prior investment in building a strong culture. And once in a while, people just drop the hint 'that the thing I like about your company is …'. That can be very satisfying.

Chapter 11

Building a coalition

In the life of every business, opportunities arise that the resources of the business alone cannot exploit. They require the business promoter to form a coalition or forge an ad hoc team to take advantage of them. The resource required may be money, landed property, business name/ licence, political influence, or bank guaranty.

My rule of thumb often is to question whether you can trust the other party. This is certainly not trust in absolute terms, but in the sense that you are familiar with the values that rule the life of the person. You don't want vain, rude, and greedy people. Even if they are offering you the best deal, when the situation gets sticky, what rises to the surface are the enduring values that rule their lives.

You should always commit agreement to the written form, including the obligations of each party and the reward for different outcomes. You should observe this even if you are dealing with your blood brother or closest friend. It is a powerful instrument of record keeping and control. Whatever you commit to writing may not cover everything, but it will surely reduce areas of contention in the future.

I have had occasions twice to argue fees due to lawyers after services rendered. One particularly alarming case was a lawyer who kept arguing against what he had committed to in writing. The other one did not dispute what we showed him, but he kept insisting that there was a higher figure agreed while being unable to provide any written evidence to support his claim. People totally change once it is payment time. Even a simple line of email may be your saving grace.

You should never be afraid to forge coalitions; in fact, it is the only way to leapfrog the business. In the process, you may be hurt or betrayed. But that comes with the territory. It is the only way you will understand human nature.

Chapter 12

Growing the business

Growth, as it is in the life of a person, is imperative in business. A business is like riding a bicycle: in order for you to maintain your stability, you have got to continue moving. Growth is necessary to keep your best staff. Growth in the business will throw up opportunity for promotions and increased responsibility for your staff. That may be enough to keep them. It is one of the motivations for staying with small companies. Growth will also be an affirmation of your hard work and a reward for your personal sacrifices and effort. It will be proof of the increased value of your business. All of your other stakeholders – regulators, banks, investors, suppliers, customers, and so forth – will also take you more seriously with visible progress, and with that comes stronger bargaining power.

The direction in which to grow should be a deliberate one, guided often by the strength and resources of the business, market opportunities, and the core business.

The initial direction of growth should be organic, using the existing resources of the business – basically human capital and intellectual property. It will come by way of taking existing products to new geographical markets or by simply increasing your offerings to existing markets by increasing your products. This kind of growth is safe, and a mistake will be easily noticeable and may not kill the company. It requires vigilance and may challenge managerial skills in areas that were previously untested. Planning, delegation, monitoring, and other skills may be tested. It requires an awareness of the fact that the company has changed, even if so slightly.

My product development company started out as a one-man company focusing solely on product development. Our marketing was outsourced. So was production. We took in marketing following a dispute on payment with our outsourcing partner. This forced a radical expansion with an additional four people and an immediate need for new cars for them. We were not ready, and we compromised on the quality of the used cars we purchased. It affected our branding, and the next growth phase – taking our products to the north of Nigeria with an additional five people in different cities of the north – was more deliberate. This was more traumatic. We stretched our cash flow, and supervision was inadequate. We lost a lot of money, and we had to disengage all of the staff we hired – a very unpleasant task.

The next phase of growth was compelled by regulatory pressures. The cost of complying with regulations by NAFDAC and the Pharmacists Council of Nigeria (PCN) was becoming prohibitive for the size of our business. Bringing the function in-house would have created a massive redundancy, as our products were too few to engage a staff full-time.

We now came to the middle-of-the-road decision of setting up a stand-alone company that will not only service our requirement for regulatory compliance but will also provide the service to other companies. This proved to be a very successful decision, as the business broke in only eighteen months and started generating cash to support the product development and marketing business. It proved a very good synergy with our original business.

Any business person, after stabilizing his or her core business and knowing that it is beginning to run a steady course, can afford to take a bigger risk. The key rule here is that any new initiative should not draw on the cash resources of the anchor business. It may share space, personnel, and/or equipment, but not cash. The reason for this is obvious: cash is scarce, and any excess should be diverted to insuring the survival of the business going forward. Yes, it can be argued that a new venture will also secure the future survival of the business. But new ventures are by nature risky, and it is important that businesses are ring-fenced, such that the failure of one does not threaten the survival of the other.

You should forever be alert to opportunities in the business environment: businesses or assets for sale, privatization, deregulation, agency opportunities for foreign businesses, divestments, and so on. Be ready to take advantage of these opportunities as long as they fit your broadly defined criteria. I bought a house in the United States during the real-estate crisis that I formed a business around, and I put it out for rent as a source of extra income. I also partook in the purchase of a financial services company in Nigeria during the economic meltdown of 2008 that led to the foreclosure of many businesses globally. The global economic crisis of 2008 threw up many opportunities that I took advantage of.

Chapter 13

Developing a cash reflex

I have discussed the imperative of cash for any business. The ultimate proof of business acumen is the cash reflex: the sixth sense to see an opportunity to make money from the most unlikely source. Combined with a capacity to manage cost, turning every opportunity to cash may give your business a new lease of life and may in fact be the difference between the life or death of the business. I learnt a lot about this interacting with my partner in the financial services business. Your licence, your business name, your business registration with a procurement agency, and other intangible assets can be leveraged for collaboration with other people to do contracts, and trade in articles that require specialized certifications.

Sola Solarin

The premises of our pharmaceutical manufacturing business came with huge unused space that we could have deployed to warehousing goods for third parties, raising another stream of income. Our facility had the capability to make the highest quality portable water for the Nigerian market at a time that that segment was growing. I guess I was too much of a pharmacist to see those opportunities.

A cash reflex also means tuning in to the banks. What kind of transactions are they financing? What is their risk appetite like? There is no point joining the bandwagon of whiners who are forever abusing the banks for not supporting particular sectors. If banks are providing short-term capital, offer them proposals with a short-term cash cycle. Develop products that will fit their risk appetite. It is not the responsibility of the entrepreneur to solve the problem of the economy. You simply structure your business to take advantage of government policy to make profit within the framework of the requirements of the providers of capital. You should see things as they are and not as you wish them to be (with credit to Jack Welch, former CEO of General Electric (GE) for that statement).

The government also provides grants and subsidies that support specific industries or influence certain behaviours. If you qualify, you should take advantage of them. For a small business, it may take quite some effort to put together an application in the right format to qualify for these government programmes. But then, there are consultants who specialize in these things and take the weight off you for a fee.

Chapter 14

Running out of cash

Empirical data shows that from 2003 to 2009 in Nigeria, loans to small and medium-sized enterprises (SMEs) as a percentage of total credits given by banks decreased from 7.45 per cent to 0.18 per cent. A total of 90 per cent of SMEs die within the first year. Only between 5 and 10 per cent survive after the first ten years and grow into corporate status.

A small business will at one point in its life run out of cash. The business could be doing well and the promoter is taking out cash to finance other projects or just plain wasting it on hedonistic sprees. It could be that the business is growing so fast that the cash need of the business far out paces its capacity to generate cash internally.

The business could have been undercapitalized from the start, and the requirements for cash crystallized soon after commencement of the business. Although I may not have empirical data, I suspect the reason for the death of most start-ups in Nigeria is caused by an effluxion of cash. It is the most toxic of all business afflictions. A business may be unprofitable and survive if it continues to have cash flow. It is the life blood of all businesses. A profitable business will, however, not survive for long without cash.

Managing cash is the most important operational task of a business promoter. Like in the words of Andy Grove of Intel fame, it is one instance where only the 'paranoids survive' when it comes to cash and business continuity.

It is good to anticipate cash requirement ahead of time. This is revealed by a cash budget at the beginning of the year. This is a task that a business promoter should never outsource or delegate. A simple cash budget is easy. Create an Excel spreadsheet showing all monthly cash inflows and outflows and the resulting cash balances at the end of the month.

If there are monthly cash shortages, the promoter must plan for find ways of augmenting the treasury with cash by borrowing or simply delaying certain projects.

If there is excess cash at the end of the period, this is when paranoia should set in. The promoter must plan ahead of time what to do with the excess cash. If excess cash is not planned for, it will be wasted on frivolities.

My usual attitude is to convert cash to other assets that are not easy to access. In Nigeria, the stock market and real estate are investments that often retain their value even in inflationary times. The stock market may be volatile at times, but if an investor knows that his or her objective is to hide cash for future use, he or she will probably only stick to liquid stocks that have a history of consistent growth. Playing the market for instant wealth is not a game he or she should play. This investor doesn't have the competence nor the infrastructure to excel in such games.

In real estate, the promoter should invest only in assets with the right titles, that is, only those with certificate of occupancy (C of O). A business promoter shouldn't allow himself or herself to be distracted by the shenanigans and trickery required to procure title from government

Sola Solarin

agencies. Other than the oil and gas industry, real estate is the other putrid hotbed of corruption in Nigeria.

The reason that I recommend stocks and real estate is because they are a good store of value and, more importantly, they are acceptable to lenders as collateral for loans. A business promoter soon finds out that there are instances in the life of a business where a lack of capacity to raise N1m can lead to the loss of an opportunity to make N10m.

Before you build capacity to acquire assets that can serve as collateral, a business may need cash. This is where you call on personal relationships – people such as your parents, your siblings, and your friends who will give you money to ensure you succeed. These are people who won't ask questions in your hour of desperate need. It is important to preserve these relationships by ensuring that you pay back the money. Because you will need them again, and if you did not abuse the relationship the last time, they will oblige you again and again and again.

There are also the short-term lenders: the finance houses, the micro-finance banks, and savings and loans companies. They charge very high interest rates, but they are very flexible with the collaterals that they take. A car, your stock of jewelleries, and simple domiciliation of proceed of a transaction are acceptable to them. The trick is not to use facilities from these kinds of institutions for longer than two months. Anything longer than that makes them too expensive and dangerous.

The lessons here are obvious. It could be dangerous – and may be fatal – for a business to run out of cash. A business promoter should be paranoid about the management of cash and should always be prepared for when cash runs out. Keep all relationships and infrastructure required for raising cash open and well oiled. It may make the difference between the life or death of the business.

Chapter 15

Enforcing contracts, collecting your money

Nigeria is the ultimate jungle when it comes to enforcement of contracts. The police are unprofessional and available for hire. The judicial system is corrupt, and cases are slow, and systems are antiquated. The system is therefore not configured to support small businesses dealing in small ticket transactions. Getting a court judgment for transactions in small sums, the remit of small businesses will require you to hire a lawyer and go to court with the possibility of never getting justice. Even if you get a judgment in your favour, you will need to finance the enforcement of the judgment. All of these factors make self-help and criminalization of commercial disputes very enticing prospects; it is often cheaper to go to the police, pay a small sum, and arrest the other party for fraud in a case of simple breach of contract. This is tedious, but it works most of the time.

A lot of businesses protect themselves by insisting on cash for every transaction. However, this doesn't work for all businesses. Real-estate rental may command upfront payment for the first three years, but subsequent rentals may fall into arrears. Some services are delivered in full after part payment. Credit transactions are inevitable, and there will be the need to resolve a payment dispute somehow.

Sometimes customers/clients will take a small business owner to court to frustrate a transaction, lleading the business down the path of unnecessary legal expenses and an indeterminate process.

I have tried to limit the damage that this can cause by including either an arbitration or other similar dispute resolution clause in all contracts no matter how inconsequential it may seem. All letters of employment issued to my employees, all invoices, and other transaction documents carry a statement that all disputes will be resolved by a binding arbitration or alternative dispute resolution (ADR) system.

I have seen this work spectacularly in a few complex commercial disputes in Nigeria. The resolution of dispute between Econet Wireless Nigeria (EWN) and Nigerian Directors was done in less than two years.

If it had gone through our normal legal system, ten years after they would still be at the supreme court arguing on jurisdiction and other inconsequential matters while the business is bleeding.

I also saw it work in the case of Hotel Support Services Limited and West African Examination Council (WAEC) on the concessioning of a hotel in Lagos. The case was resolved in less than two months.

Chapter 16

Scams everywhere

When foreigners claim that they fell victim to article 419 of the Nigerian Criminal Code fraud because they responded to an invitation to partake in a transaction by email, many Nigerians are surprised because the average business person is wired to smell a scam from 10 kilometres away. A story about wanting to use an account to launder the proceeds of a crime, for which you will earn so many millions of dollars, has little chance of success with the small business promoter in Nigeria.

The more successful scammers of small businesses are people using the authority and power of government agencies to perpetrate fraud. Sometimes it is done with the active connivance and participation of the leadership of the agencies. The average Nigerian still trusts, venerates, and fears people in power. And it is so easy to bury complaints about government officials in the bureaucracy. Our public officials and politicians tend to get away with malfeasance like this, and it is becoming very popular. Worse still the complainant/victim of the scam may now become a target of persecution by the government official/agency perpetrating the fraud. There are, however, other means of bringing them to justice.

A very famous case was that of an agency regulating a critical sector in social services in Nigeria. When a new chief executive was appointed, he turned out to be the protégé of a very notorious politician. He showed his hand immediately by amending the procedure for renewal of and taking out new applications for product regulation. Embedded in this new procedure was a requirement to prove the status of your company registration with the Corporate Affairs Commission (the central registry for businesses in Nigeria and a sister government department). However, this new chief executive decreed that the only proof acceptable to the agency must be one from a law firm named by the agency in the new guidelines.

The motivation behind this sleight of hand was so ridiculously obvious that only an incredibly stupid person could have thought that it would succeed.

There are cheaper and more open methods of ascertaining a registration status. Banks do it regularly whenever you want to open a corporate account. For an extra charge of about US$30, the banks check the status of your registration at the CAC. Besides, this is a sister government agency, and they can easily provide the information required at practically no cost. A requirement of the submission of a tax clearance certificate or proof of filing of annual returns would also have been proof of the status of every business.

The industry association affected was very mature in its approach to handling this issue. Without being confrontational, the industry just said that even if it had to pay for this service, it was only willing to pay the agency directly. The agency could then forward the money to the nominated law firm. The chief executive was smart enough to see the booby traps that this represented. The rules guiding the employment of service providers to government agencies and the innumerable controls on public accounts thwarted the shenanigans of the leadership of the agency. He abandoned that requirement totally.

The same chief executive tried the same scam when the agency wanted to register consultants who will be dealing with the agency. This time, nothing was put in writing. A phone call was advertised for further enquiries. Potential consultants who called the number were told to send their application and payment to a private company whose particulars were provided and that the private company would be collecting fees for a job (evaluation and appointment of consultants) being done by a government agency.

Dealing with consultants that had no industry association and therefore no lobby group was thought to be easy; they had no voice and were possibly incapable of protesting. This initiative was as much a scam as any other.

Individual consultants simply put the facts in writing and sent the details to different anti-corruption news portals with wide followership.

When applicants moved to pay, they were advised to hold on for a subsequent directive. The subsequent directive was now that payment should be made directly to the agency's account. This is similar to what happened at the Ministry of Interior (MOI) when they employed immigration officials, a job that the ministry and the immigration service had competently done over the years. It was, however, outsourced to a private company whose ownership was eventually traced to a political office holder with a long history of corrupt practices. Sale of forms alone fetched the company almost a billion naira, and the poorly supervised process led to the deaths of several applicants.

A federal government development bank does not have cash to deploy as a loan. Yet it kept encouraging small business owners to apply for a loan. Afterwards, the fund asked that they contribute N500,000 as counterpart funding for the loan. The loan never materialized. There was no money to advance as loan. This was known to the management of the fund, yet it continued fleecing small businesses. This kind of scam is the ultimate heist. Getting a reprieve is outright impossible, and it is the stock in trade of most government institutions.

Chapter 17

Regulatory agencies and government policy

Legend has it that a very prominent lady industrialist was talking with the president of the Federal Republic of Nigeria during a coffee break from a meeting at the State House. And, as is customary, the president asked how things are going in her sector. The lady responded that the head of one of the regulatory agencies overseeing the sector was pursuing a policy that was inimical to progress of players in the industry. The president took notice. When next he met with the head of this regulatory agency, the president casually mentioned what had been related, and the agency practically rolled back the implementation of the initiative in question.

The initiative was supposed to be the cornerstone of a multitude of solutions for controlling product faking. A lot of new businesses had invested money and effort perfecting a solution, and it was going to open up a huge market that would take advantage of the needs of the market. A casual discussion on the corridor simply put paid to a government policy, and, alongside that, wasted huge investment by entrepreneurs hoping to give life and meaning to such a policy.

In the Nigerian context, this situation is by no means peculiar, although it was not helped by a leadership in the agency that could not argue its convictions (if at all there was any) and with a political ambition that may not be helped by any sign of obstinacy.

Policies and regulations are often initiated on the whims of the leadership of regulatory agencies. They feel no need to test concepts, prove that an idea works, and secure stakeholders' buy-in before pushing for implementation. The public service with its history of supervision by a hierarchical and dictatorial military government and culture of unquestioning obeisance to authority treats the leaders of regulatory agencies like gods. Policies therefore don't enjoy the test of challenge from robust public debate and empiricism. They arrive weak and unproven, and they often collapse like a house built on sand.

The moral of the story is that even though huge profits and a multitude of opportunities come with a new order of things wrought by new government policies, no small business should stake resources it cannot afford to lose on a government policy. In the Nigeria situation, a very powerful executive arm of government and a weak bureaucracy makes the evolution of policy a very uncertain process. Policy can be truncated at any point. It may even be upturned after public announcement and commencement of implementation. Even when a policy has been successfully adopted, the system is weak at enforcing laws and regulations. The full benefits of the regulation may not be available to those who depend on it for business success. It is therefore inadvisable for a small business not to base its business strategy on government policy.

Chapter 18

Personal development

For a small business owner, personal development is an imperative. It helps boost confidence and validates the conscious choice of going solo. It is not inferior to working with a big organization. It is simply a different choice that will take you down a different trajectory. Personal development helps you keep things in perspective and develop skills that are important for business success.

Social media (such as Facebook, LinkedIn, and Twitter) and a host of other options keep you abreast by the minute on developments in your industry and around the world. They require, however, careful calibration in order to prevent information overload and the constant irritation that frequent update alerts can constitute. Besides, they are also invaluable marketing and promotional tools for your business, products, and person.

Subscription to newsfeeds from newspaper portals and agency reports are also useful.

For the small business owner, a course in the use of social media would be a good investment.

Take your hobby to the next level – be it cycling, fitness, reading, volunteering, public advocacy, religion, or public speaking. Whatever your interest is, you will find people organized and promoting and pursuing that hobby. It exposes you immediately to a community where you don't need any effort to start a conversation with the individual members and ultimately bond at the individual and business level. Create the time to join a committee in the group. It makes for closer bonding and pushes the relationship from acquaintanceship to friendship. Anything can happen from there.

Join your industry groups, one professional and one pressure group. Attend one conference a year. Decide on your personal brand and communicate it in your introduction. A short, simple answer to, 'What do you do?' or, 'Who are you?; should be one like, 'I sell books', 'Pharmaceutical compliance services', 'I am in truck haulage', 'I am in men's fashion', 'Social media marketing', or 'Executive recruitment'. Join a committee in your professional group as well. It keeps you in touch and helps with personal bonding with people. Try to write an article for a newspaper or industry journal, or deliver a talk once a year.

In all of these, never lose sight of the opportunity to take advantage of these relationships for your business. Never seek undue advantage. Compete fairly, and maintain integrity in your relationships. If you lose, you will learn a lesson; if you win, make sure that no one regrets doing business with you.

Chapter 19

International collaboration: embracing Asia

Even while conceptualizing the manufacturing business early in my entrepreneurial life, Asian countries, notably India and China, already loomed large, and I knew that there was no way that the business would be competitive without sourcing some inputs from Asia.

The Asians have benefited the healthcare system, and I dare say the entire economy in more ways than one. China and India have perfected the art of low-cost manufacturing. Helped by a large local market, albeit a poor one, factories in this region stretched the concept of economy of scale and vertical integration to its limit and were constantly churning out in huge volumes cheap manufactured goods that have thankfully kept prices low and improved standard of living. In the pharmaceutical sector where World Trade Organization (WTO) regulations and patent laws kept newer and better medicines out of the reach of the majority of the populace in low-income countries, people were condemned to certain deaths in the worst cases or a painful and compromised existence because of an inability to afford required remedies.

China and India were late signatories to the WTO pact, and they insisted on the right to manufacture medicines locally in spite of patent protection. New remedies for treatment of human immunodeficiency virus (HIV) and acquired immune deficiency syndrome (AIDS), although still under patent, were manufactured in Asia and then filtered into the African market at a fraction of the prices that they would be available from Western multinationals. In the early 1990s, a company I was working for was selling a one-month course of a medicine for HIV/AIDS treatment at about five times the minimum wage. By the end of that decade, thanks to an improved version of the same class of drugs from companies in Asia, the cost of a month's course of treatment had plummeted to one-third of the minimum wage.

The same scenario played out in the market for raw material and other inputs into the production process. Finished goods and raw materials were coming at compellingly low prices from the East, and management literature was celebrating businesses like Nike and Apple that built their business model on outsourcing manufacturing to Asia. It was therefore a no brainer to look East in search of manufacturing inputs. But there were a few concerns.

Asia had a long-running reputation for base business ethics and a proclivity to deliberately produce substandard product. A judicial system like Nigeria's made enforcement of contract difficult. The options open to Nigerian businesses were to travel to China or India and supervise the loading and shipment of their orders and hand over cash on completion of transactions – and this of course was not feasible for small orders – or to place an order on a European country that would source from Asia and deliver the required materials to Lagos.

Our preference at the beginning was to choose a European procurement company with global operations to handle our orders. They had an indenting office in Lagos, and they would take full responsibility for the quality of the product and the commercial terms of the contract. The arrangement worked perfectly for us, albeit at a premium for very obvious reasons.

However, the lure of lower prices proved irresistible, and on recommendation of some trusted friends we started dealing directly with a company in China. Everything worked well for four years; orders were delivered expeditiously, and they were often prompt in attending to any issue.

The values of the company in China were put to test when a batch of raw material supplied failed laboratory testing. We went across with the laboratory test results and a request for what we should do. They promised to investigate at their end, but they came back with an insistence that the material was OK, in spite of very obvious physical evidence to the contrary. We reported to the commercial attaché of the embassy in Lagos, who acknowledged with a phone call and promised to investigate. It was the last we heard from either the company or the Chinese consulate in Lagos.

What was most galling about this incident was the change in attitude of the company representative as soon as the report on the quality of the defective product batch was made. Gone was the very solicitous and friendly tone. Her manners became defensive and formal, and she in fact queried our competence to pass judgement on the quality of materials. China was about 12,000 kilometres away at a cost of US$3,000 air fare (in economy class). It was pointless contemplating legal action.

The incident forced us to write off the material, kept us out of the market for about six months at a critical time in the lifecycle of the product, and hastened our decision to exit the product business. The moral of this story is that for business risks you have no control over, it is better to pay a little more for service providers with solid pedigrees and an enforceable grievance resolution process.

Chapter 20

Making the call

There are times when having given your best efforts, stretched yourself to the limit, and liquidated assets that you can afford, you get to your wits' end. The market has turned, the competitive environment has changed, the fundamentals of the market are no longer the same, and you are piling losses upon losses, and you simply can't compete anymore. It is time to make the call: Should you sell? Should you scale down? Should you shut down?

This moment requires as much courage as you summoned when you started the business. You owe a few people some explanations – chief among which being your spouse and your shareholders. This moment of epiphany often comes after passing through the four stages of grief;

a denial that this is not happening to a business you've mastered and successfully ran for a while; depression that you've wasted such a valuable and productive part of your life on a project that is failing, and inability to see any light at the end of the long, dark tunnel; anger that the world is so unfair and had simply refused to reward your valiant efforts and sacrifices; and, finally, acceptance that you need to pack it up. Or do you?

In spite of the hopelessness of the situation, all of the assets of the business haven't disappeared. You still have a reputation in the industry, industry knowledge, licences and certifications, brands, franchises, and a host of other things. You can put them all together in a way that makes you fall forward. There are still a few options open to you.

Sell

You can sell the business as a going concern, with all the assets and liabilities. However, for you to have come to this decision, the business could have run such losses that the balance sheet is very unattractive and may lead to low – or even negative – valuation of the business. Also, most business owners have a few personal assets in the name of the business – such as shareholding in other companies, real-estate interest, and the family car – that they may not want to sell with the business.

The option to sell as a going concern can be a necessary one compelled by the industry and the prevailing regulatory regime.

Scale down

You may choose to scale down. You may reduce activities to the bare essentials and simply maintain enough infrastructure to retain licences, certifications, approvals, and all that is necessary to remain in business. This is a state of hibernation, with your antennae tuned to sense opportunities for a quick buck or a changing environment that will enable you to come back to business. You can also adopt this state to await a more opportune time to sell the business at a better value.

Shut down

The last option is of course total liquidation of the business: sale of assets as scrap, non-renewal of certifications, non-renewal of licences, and no new address – not even to receive mails. This may be an option if it costs more to even maintain a business as a shell than shutting it down. Our financial services business ended up like that. The cost of maintaining staff and auditors to simply keep up with filing quarterly returns to the regulatory authorities was simply too heavy to bear.

Chapter 21

You did not fail

Management literature is filled with examples of businesses that look nothing like how they started out. Less than fifty years ago Nokia was a pulp and paper company. It rode the crest of the introduction of the mobile phone industry to become the largest producer of mobile phone handsets in the world. It was blindsided by the creative genius of Steve Jobs, CEO of Apple Inc, and the low-cost manufacturing excellence of Samsung. It is today a manufacturer of telecommunications equipment servicing mobile phone companies. NCR Corporation (formally National Cash Register), the American company, started as a manufacturer of cash registers, and it evolved into a manufacturer of computers before settling to making and supporting automatic/

automated teller machines (ATM) today. These companies have assured their immortality by constantly changing with the times, and their founders will not recognize them in their present state. This is true of small businesses as it is of big companies. It doesn't matter if they are in developed economies or emerging countries.

Your small business needs to be nimble and quick to recognize changes in the environment and adapt very quickly.

Shutting down a business that can no longer compete is not failure. It is pragmatism. Even if you lost the battle, you would have learnt a lesson. That in itself is invaluable.

Chapter 22

Government role in enabling small business

The case for an agenda for the Small and Medium-Sized Enterprise(SME) is compelling and self-evident. They constitute about 40 per cent of the Nigerian economy. According to the Federal Ministry of Industry, Trade and Investment, small and medium-sized businesses number more than 17 million. The potential to generate employment is enormous if each SME employs just one additional hand. The most recent published data from the National Bureau of Statistics (NBS) revealed that 62 per cent of all the employment generated in the last quarter of 2014 was consequent of the informal sector (read small business). Its capacity to maintain social order also becomes stark when you read the narrative about the remote cause of the xenophobic attacks in South Africa. Foreigners have pushed the natives out of the small business space.

The Nigerian is configured for small business. Right from infancy, the Yorubas hone it into the psyche of little ones that failure is refusing to devote oneself to either education or a trade. The Igbos indenture young ones to the care of successful family members to learn a trade. The suya barbeque stand and the neighbourhood money changer cannot be anyone else but a Hausa man. All over the world, in the taxis of New York, the market stalls in Abidjan, the corner shops in Johannesburg, the itinerant real-estate agent in Atlanta, and the African restaurants in London, Nigerians wake up early to eke out a living plying trades that fetch pennies and cents per transaction.

The small business owner has survived in spite of government. The new government in Nigeria, in enlightened self-interest, has to pay attention to SMEs in order to achieve some quick wins and sustain the goodwill that swept it into office. A few enablers are what small businesses need to thrive and build on the momentum that has been powering this economy for the last ten years.

The railway was the life blood of the pre-independence economy. Cities and lives were nurtured on the regular, rhythmic chugs of locomotives drawing along rolling stocks with their payload of passengers, agricultural produce, industrial raw material, minerals, and construction materials. Cities like Abeokuta, Zungeru, Osogbo, Kontagora, and Zaria as well as many others achieved fame and prominence in the early history of Nigeria because of the railways. The system was narrow gauge and slow. It was, however, consistent and reliable, and business could plan their logistics around it. Today's small business doesn't need the bullet trains of Japan to add two full points to our GDP. The immediate requirement of small business today is a consistent rail service, not a faster one. If a trader can be sure that a train will depart Lagos at noon every day and arrive in Kaduna, which is about 800 kilometres away, twenty-four hours later and in Maiduguri forty-eight hours later, he can build an economy around it, broaden the reach of his or her products, and, more importantly, avoid the greatest threat to enterprise in Nigeria today, namely, government agents (mainly police officers and local government revenue officers). This can only be achieved if government concession the maintenance of the tracks to private companies. Any one that can buy locomotives and rolling stocks should have access to the tracks, subject of course to abiding by extant regulations. It should suck in the required investments and expertise.

The case for a regular electricity supply has been made many times over. Its enabler role can only be compared to what we are presently experiencing with telecommunications. It has made banking as we know it today possible and also a more credible electoral system. Imagine what stable electricity will do to the fishers, the butchers, the barbers, and the welders, or the fresh graduate doing simple software designs in the computer village in Ikeja. We can only imagine.

Lagos has found a way of taxing small business in a simple but effective way. Taxi drivers are licensed and pay N10,000 yearly for renewal. Every market stall pays N2,000 monthly. Every artisan or trader pays one levy or the other. We need to bring such simplicity and sanity to small businesses employing less than ten people. At present any business with the ambition to formalize will need to build a whole bureaucracy to cope with government levies and taxes. With a staff complement of just three people, a small business will need to pay make payments for an industrial training fund, a pension, health insurance, personal income tax for its staff, a social insurance fund, withholding tax, company income tax, value-added tax, education tax, and a sundry of other mandatory insurances. It is simply more convenient to operate below the radar, not disclose the full complement of staff, and remain perpetually small. I will suggest that any business making below N50m in revenue should simply pay a flat fee, and there should be tangible benefits accruable to compliance beyond the harassment by government agents.

Government-assisted access to finance, business continuity insurance, or health insurance are benefits that could make this attractive.

Access to credit is the fourth critical enabler. The Soludo era at the Central Bank of Nigeria (CBN) was the glory days of access to credit to small business. This was not achieved by direct intervention as presently favoured by the present regime, but rather through a deft manipulation of monetary and fiscal levers that made the Treasury bill rate low, and therefore unattractive as an investment instrument. Liquidity in the system was high, and money was available and looking for investment outlets. Inflation was in low double digits, but we could live with that. The banks became creative in developing products for small businesses using cash flow and a business plan as 'collateral'. Economic growth powered into the 7 to 8 per cent range, and everyone benefited. I think our banks are sophisticated enough to pick viable projects from SMEs for funding. They must, however, be compelled by the market to make that choice. A CBN with a developmental mind-set that trusts the market can make this happen.

Our mechanics, masons, shoe makers, chefs/cooks, welders, and other artisans are being left behind by technology. Their masters were trained before the advent of computer technology and the ubiquitous use of fibreglass. They simply passed on their antiquated knowledge. They were never taught about cash books, and they don't know how to raise an invoice or the meaning of a receipt. The fifth enabler, training, requires more elaborate work, but the pay-off in the long run is immense. The first thing to do is to remodel artisanal training. Tuition should be conducted in local languages. It should incorporate new developments in their trade and simple record keeping of business activities. The difference between labour and materials should be emphasized, as well as why it is not necessary – and possibly unethical – to mix the two. Presenting the training modules on DVDs will improve the reach. Some level of certification will help. This will give value and dignity to their calling.

This economy still has a lot of scope for growth. It requires an appreciation of the potential of the SMEs to unleash it.

www.ingramcontent.com/pod-product-compliance
Lightning Source LLC
Chambersburg PA
CBHW030859180526
45163CB00004B/1639